A Day To Remember

The following stories are based on actual people, places and animals. However, some names, characters and incidents have been created for dramatic purposes.

www.hippobooks.info

Hippo Books is a publisher dedicated to publishing fun and readable books in English. Our books are ideal for improving your English reading and comprehension skills.

Table of Contents

The Last Song

Part One

Wallace Hartley settled into his bunk on the Titanic. Wallace was the band leader of the Titanic's eight piece orchestra. He was in the second-class passenger rooms, just above the library. He lived in a room with Roger Bricoux, a twenty year old French cellist. It was amazing to Wallace how energetic Roger was; the Frenchman never shut up about his time studying in Italy, or his previous voyages.

Just now, Roger was talking in heavily-accented English about a woman he had seen in the second class diner. 'She was so beautiful,' he said. 'I almost told her in French, "Bonjour mon mignon!"'

'I'm sure you did,' Wallace said, settling onto his bunk. He took out a cigarette, lit it, and took a deep drag, watching the smoke float up to the metal ceiling. Wallace had been playing on cruise ships for three years. It was an easy life, apart from the fact that he was always at sea.

The Titanic was the largest ship in the world at the time. The ship had a gymnasium, a Turkish bath, a Parisian café and several restaurants. Still, Wallace didn't completely trust the ocean, no matter how large the Titanic was.

Roger started speaking rapidly in French. He was walking back and forth across the small room, showing

Wallace a dance move. He was very dramatic, but sometimes he was ridiculous; Wallace enjoyed the Frenchman's company in the morning, but he was a little irritating at bedtime.

He looked out of the porthole in their room. The Atlantic Ocean was black and silky; the dark waves reflecting thousands of stars. How many mysteries did the sea hold? How many strange and beautiful creatures were under the Titanic right now, swimming in the darkness?

The size of the sea always surprised Wallace; it seemed to be never-ending. He liked to wake up before dawn and go up on deck. The sight of the sun rising over the water always filled his heart with warmth.

'Hey, are you listening to me?' Roger asked.

'Sorry,' Wallace said. He put his cigarette out in the ashtray. 'I was thinking about something.'

'What were you thinking about?' Roger asked.

'The sea.'

'Why do you think about the sea? It is big and it is blue. There's nothing more than that except for some very big fish!' He laughed at his own joke.

'The sea is mysterious,' Wallace said. 'It connects

everything in the world together. At the same time, the sea ignores everything that happens to mankind. It observes but never judges.'

'Ah! You feel like a philosopher tonight, eh?' Roger sat down on his bunk. 'My grandfather was a philosopher.'

'Was he?'

'Yes, if you gave him some wine, he would tell you about many things! He would talk for hours without stopping.' The Frenchman suddenly looked sad. 'He died five years ago.'

'How?' Wallace asked with concern.

'Too much philosophy!' he said, laughing.

'Good night, Roger.' He turned away from the young Frenchman. They had several concerts to play the next day and he was tired. He fell into a deep sleep to the rocking of the giant ship on the waves.

Part Two

The next day was mostly uneventful. The orchestra played a few concerts and people enjoyed themselves. Everyone on the Titanic seemed to be having fun. The people in first class lived in luxury, eating delicious food and sleeping in five-star cabins. The people in second and third class had the view of the ocean and each other's company, but that was good enough.

That night, the band set up in the first class Parisian café to perform. Wallace led the band, playing his violin expertly. He glanced over at Roger to make sure he was playing along correctly. The Frenchman was sometimes a little wild, but that didn't matter, he was a really good musician. The other band members, Theo, George, Percy and three men who were all named John, played very well that night. The crowd clapped and some people asked them to play more songs.

Once the band finished, Wallace stepped outside to smoke a cigarette. He was joined by one of the Johns - John Law Hume. He also played the violin in the orchestra.

'It's chilly tonight,' John said, pulling his jacket tight. He was a very thin man with brown hair. He was wearing a smart black suit and a red tie.

'I noticed that,' Wallace replied. Wind blew across the deck of the ship, whipping at the flags.

'Do you think the weather will be bad tomorrow?' John asked, taking a cigarette from Wallace.

'No,' he replied. 'It will be fine.'

Wallace was wrong: it wasn't warm the next day. In fact, it was even colder than the previous night. He woke early in the morning as he normally did. After getting dressed, he walked upstairs to watch the sunrise. On the ship's deck, he ran into a sailor he knew called Clive.

'What's happening with the weather?' Wallace asked.

'A cold front came in last night,' Clive said. He was a stocky man with big arms. 'It always does this when we come to this part of the ocean.'

'Which part is this?' Wallace asked. He wondered how anyone could tell the difference in the ocean: it looked the same everywhere.

'We are approaching the Grand Banks of Newfoundland.'

'Ah,' Wallace said, turning back to the water, none the wiser.

'This can be a dangerous area to sail through.'

'Why's that?' he asked.

'Sometimes parts of glaciers break off and icebergs float under the surface of the water.'

'Really? Should I be worried?' Wallace didn't like the sound of huge lumps of ice floating underneath the ship.

'No, cruise ships go through here all the time. The Titanic can easily break through a glacier. It might shake the boat, but that's about it. Don't worry. Well, I'd better get back to work.'

Clive turned and walked towards the back of the ship with a rope under his arm. He waved over his shoulder at Wallace. A cold wind blew across the water. The enormous ship creaked slightly and continued its journey forward. Wallace finished his cigarette and went back to his room. He found Roger snoring loudly.

'Wake up,' he said to Roger.

'What?' Roger started speaking in French. Wallace ignored him. He knew some French, but not enough to understand what Roger was saying. The Frenchman sat up in his bed. He stretched his hands in front of him and yawned. 'Why did you wake me up?' he asked.

'I thought you might enjoy eating with the band this morning. We agreed to meet for breakfast, remember?'

'What?' Roger laughed. His hair was messy and his eyes were dark. 'Impossible! I would never agree to an early breakfast! Why would you think this?'

'OK, go back to sleep then.' Wallace began changing his shirt.

Roger yawned. 'On second thought, I think I will join you. I haven't had a good breakfast in ages.'

The ship creaked again and Wallace thought about what Clive had said about passing over icebergs. He decided then not to worry about the Titanic anymore. It was a big and powerful ship made of metal; there was no way a lump of ice could stop it.

Part Three

The orchestra played until midnight. People danced and cheered for them to play more. Wallace stood in front of the passengers of the Titanic and bowed. He was wearing his favorite three piece suit and a bow tie. A woman wearing an expensive looking fur coat and a diamond necklace approached him from the audience.

'Please, sir, one more song,' she said, winking at him. She was wearing a beautiful red dress and gold high heels.

He turned back to the orchestra to find Roger grinning at him. 'You heard the lady,' he said, ignoring Frenchman's smile, 'let's play another song. A slow one this time.'

They began playing a slow ballad. There was suddenly a loud bang. Wallace looked over at Roger. Roger shrugged and kept playing along.

There was another bang and then a loud creaking noise. Before Wallace could react, the boat lurched forward. People fell to the floor alongside tables and glasses. Waiters dropped their trays and tumbled over. The lights on the ceiling swung back and forth. A loud, horrible sound travelled through the metal walls. Wallace fell to his knees with his violin clutched to his chest.

An iceberg. Wallace knew what it was immediately. He didn't know how he knew, but he knew that the sound, that horrible sound which had sent shivers through everyone in the room, came from beneath the Titanic. He looked over at Roger. The Frenchman was no longer grinning; he was lying under his cello, terrified.

There was another loud noise. It sounded like the roar of some dying beast. Wallace ran over to Roger and lifted the cello off his body.

'What's happening?' Roger asked, his eyes filled with fear.

'We…'

Wallace wasn't a liar. He didn't know for a fact that they'd hit an iceberg, but he knew that something was terribly wrong.

'The boat has hit something... something big.'

'This is very bad!'

John appeared behind him with his violin. There was a little blood on his forehead from where he had hit his head on a music stand.

'Are you OK?' Wallace asked.

'I'm fine,' John assured him. He took a handkerchief from his jacket pocket and wiped his forehead. The ship suddenly lurched and rolled to one side. The floor was now slightly tilted.

Wallace checked to make sure the other band members were not injured. Everyone seemed to be all right. Passengers were running madly through the room, screaming and crying. Some of the waiters were helping the older passengers. The ship continued to tilt and creak. The lights started snapping off the ceiling and falling to the floor.

'We need to get out of here!' Roger shouted above the noise.

'Is it sinking?' John asked.

'I don't know,' Wallace said. 'We need to get on deck and see what the sailors are saying. Bring your instruments.'

'Why?' Roger and John asked together.

'Gentlemen, I'm afraid our night has just started. Hurry!'

A giant chandelier dropped from the ceiling. It landed near Wallace and his men. Glass shattered into the air; more screams reached their ears. Wallace led the orchestra through the chaos to the back of the room, where there was a staircase to the upper deck.

Part Four

Wallace's heart nearly stopped once they arrived on deck. Everyone was panicking, even some of the sailors. The Titanic had started to tilt, which could only mean one thing: the ship was sinking. The air was filled with screams. The ocean waves lashed at the sides of the great ship. Cold water splashed onto the deck causing people to slip and fall.

'The ship is sinking!' Roger screamed.

'That's impossible!' John cried.

Wallace turned to his small orchestra. The seven men looked at him for answers. He was their leader, and they trusted that he knew what to do next. But Wallace didn't know what to do. He was as terrified as they were.

'What should we do?' Roger cried. He was speaking to himself in French now. It was clear that he was very frightened.

'I…' Wallace wanted to say, "I don't know". Instead, he picked up his violin and began to play.

He played alone for a moment, a soft ballad meant to soothe the fleeing passengers. It was a very sad song, almost too sad for words. The music floated into the air, beautiful and calm. Some of the passengers stopped when they heard the music and turned to see where it was coming from. It was very strange to hear such beautiful music in all the chaos.

Soon, John began playing alongside him. He was followed by Theo, George, Percy and the other two Johns. Roger was the last to join the group. The Titanic was sinking and Wallace knew that this was the only way to help the passengers. If the orchestra played calm music, it would make the passengers less afraid.

As he played his violin, he watched sailors lower small boats full of people into the water. It was heart-breaking to see people so afraid. The cold wind lashed at the boats; the ocean was unforgiving. Just two hours ago, everyone was having a nice dinner. Now, they were trying to escape from a sinking ship. He heard a loud creak beneath his feet; the Titanic started to tilt even more.

The musicians didn't say anything to each other. They used their instruments to speak. Even Roger was quiet. They kept playing their tunes as people moved past them. Their music was helping. People were calming down. Fear was heavy in the air, but there was nothing anyone could do to change it. They continued playing their instruments as the Titanic sank into the ocean. It was a terrible night, a night that seemed as if it would never end.

Morning came six hours later, but the ship was gone. The sky was grey and filled with gloom; silence had settled over the ocean. Crates and other items that had been on the Titanic floated on top of the water… and there, floating next to one of the crates, was a violin with the initials W.H. just visible on the back.

The Search for the Boy King

Part One

Howard Carter watched the sun rise over the barren hills of the Sahara Desert in southern Egypt, the place that had been his home for the last twenty-five years. He hadn't slept at all... how could he? Today was the culmination of years of work. What occurred on this day could mean him being remembered as one of the greatest archaeologists in history; on the other hand, it could make him an international laughing stock.

Carter put on his glasses and looked once more at the telegram from Lord Carnarvon that he had received the day before. Carnarvon, an elderly English aristocrat, was the man who was paying Carter to search for the lost tomb of Pharaoh Tutankhamun. It simply said that he and his daughter, Lady Evelyn Herbert, were arriving in the morning. Carnarvon had been very patient with Carter. They had started looking for the tomb of the Boy King, as Tutankhamun was known, nearly fifteen years before.

It wasn't that Carter was bad at his job, he had found the tombs of several other pharaohs , but they had all been empty: tomb robbers had always beaten him to the prize. He had found some tombs with valuables inside, but they were not the tombs of pharaohs. This was his last chance to find an intact pharaoh's tomb… the thing that everyone in Egypt was desperate to find at that time.

Tutankhamun had ruled Egypt for only a short time before his death at age eighteen or nineteen. He had reigned over 3,000 years ago, making him one of the more ancient rulers that was thought to be buried in the Valley of the Kings. Many people had searched for his tomb, but all had failed… including Carter.

Carter checked his watch. It was 7.32am. He needed to have a wash and eat something before collecting Carnarvon and his daughter and taking them to what he hoped was the tomb of the Boy King… it was, after all, still sealed at that moment... so no one knew what was inside.

Part Two

'So why is everyone so fascinated with this 'boy king'?' asked Lady Evelyn Herbert. She was only twenty-three and far more interested in the social scene in London than ancient Egyptian kings.

'Well, it's not so much him as his tomb,' said Carter, smiling. He had known Lady Evelyn nearly all her life and had great affection for her.

'Is it full of treasure?' Evelyn clapped her hands together and leaned forward in her seat.

'That's what we are going to find out, Evelyn,' said Lord Carnarvon in a slightly irritated voice. 'Hopefully, Mr Carter has found an intact pharonic tomb… something that is similar to finding a needle in a haystack.'

Carter smiled and leaned back in his seat. The three English people were in the back of a car travelling from the city of Luxor to the burial site in the Valley of the Kings. Carter looked out of the window at the passing sand-dunes. He was not a religious man but he prayed silently that the tomb was intact.

Two days before, one of the Egyptian diggers that Carter employed had found the entrance to a tomb. After hours of excavation, they revealed a set of stone steps leading down to a sealed entrance. It was definitely a tomb, but whose tomb was it? And was it intact or had it been robbed and resealed by tomb raiders? There was only one way to find out.

The car went around a bend and suddenly the Valley of the Kings stretched out before them. The valley was a huge rocky expanse.

Carter had spent half of his life digging through the rock and, frankly, he was tired of it. This fatigue, coupled with Carnarvon's warning that he was no longer prepared to fund any more searching, meant that Carter was ready to give up looking for Tutankhamun's tomb if this turned out to be the tomb of another ancient aristocrat or nobleman.

'Well, I see what you mean about looking for a needle in a haystack,' said Lady Evelyn. 'It's huge.' She had come to Egypt several times with her father, but she had never visited the Valley of the Kings before.

'Yes, it was the main burial site for pharaohs and nobles for a thousand years,' replied Carter, holding on to the side of the car as it descended the bumpy road down into the valley.

‘They think that thirty-seven pharaohs were buried here,’ said Carnarvon, turning to his daughter.

‘Wow! And how many of them have been found?’ asked Evelyn.

‘Thirty-six,’ said Carter.

Part Three

‘Well, here we are,’ said Carter as they pulled up next to the rocky side of the valley.

‘It’s so close to the cliffs,’ said Carnarvon.

‘Yes, that’s one of the reasons it took us so long to find it.’ Carter looked up at the rocks towering above him. ‘We were looking in the middle of the valley; we didn’t think to look at the sides.’

‘Why did they bury him here, so close to the cliffs,’ asked Evelyn. She was becoming more and more interested as the day progressed.

‘For just this reason,’ said Carter. ‘He was almost impossible to find. Tomb robbers are not a new thing in Egypt; even back when Tutankhamun was king, there were still people who wanted to steal his treasure.’

‘Well, why would he need treasure anyway?’ asked Evelyn as they started to walk up the hill towards the entrance to the tomb. ‘He was *dead*, after all.’

‘The Egyptians didn’t believe in death in the same way that we do, darling,’ said Carnarvon. He was breathing heavily and sweating; he was no longer a young man.

'That's right,' replied Carter, taking Carnarvon's arm and helping him up the hill. 'The Egyptians believed very strongly in an after-life. If your body was disturbed, then your spirit would not travel freely to paradise.'

'But, aren't we going to disturb him now?' asked Evelyn, suddenly concerned.

'Well, yes, I suppose we are,' replied Carter. 'But I imagine that his spirit is safe in paradise by now.'

'Let's hope so,' said Evelyn.

They reached the top of the stone staircase. It led down into darkness. 'Well, here we are,' said Carter. His heart was beating hard and his hands were sweaty. Carter was usually cool in difficult situations, but even he was feeling the huge amount of pressure and expectation. Although they were the only people there except for a couple of Egyptian diggers, the world would hear about what happened next – good or bad.

'Yes, here we are,' said Carnarvon. The ageing aristocrat was also feeling the weight of expectation. Many people, including his wife, had told him that he was wasting his money looking for the tomb of Tutankhamun. Even if he did find it, they said, it would be empty like all the others.

Carter lit a candle and took Lady Evelyn's hand. The three of them descended the steps into the gloom below. At the bottom of the staircase, there was a stone wall.

'This is the entrance.' Carter took a hammer and chisel from his pocket and handed them to Lord Carnarvon. 'I'd like you to open the door, sir.'

‘No, Carter, you should do it.’ Carnarvon smiled and pushed the tools back to Carter.

‘Thank you, sir.’ Carter took the chisel, a tool that his grand-mother had given him on his seventeenth birthday, and made a small hole. It was easier than he thought it would be. He then used the hammer to make a larger hole. His heart was now racing. He took the candle and poked his head inside the tomb.

‘Well?’ asked Carnarvon, impatiently. ‘Can you see anything?’

‘Yes,’ said Carter. He removed his head from the hole. He had a huge smile on his dusty face. ‘Wonderful things.’

Part Four

‘Yes!’ cried Carnarvon. ‘Let’s get inside and have a look then!’

‘Good idea, sir!’ Carter started to break down the wall with his hammer. The air inside was ancient and smelled terrible. The three of them stood back for a minute to allow fresh air from outside to enter the tomb.

‘Let’s go,’ said Evelyn. She couldn’t wait a second longer.

Once inside, they could see the extent of the treasures and valuables. There were life-size horses of solid gold; ebony and ivory sculptures; chariots; two huge gold thrones; bracelets, necklaces, rings and earrings; and hundreds of jewels of different colours, shapes and sizes.

Carnarvon stood with his mouth open. ‘This must be worth millions of pounds,’ he whispered.

‘Oh yes, sir, millions and millions.’ Carter walked to the wall and shone his candle on some paintings. They looked as if they had been painted yesterday, not 3,000 years ago. ‘Beautiful,’ he whispered.

‘This is the find of the century, Carter!’ said Carnarvon, walking among the treasures, his wide eyes shining in the light from his candle.

‘Yes, but where is he?’ asked Evelyn, examining a ruby the size of a golf ball.

‘Who?’ asked Carnarvon, distractedly.

‘Tutankhamun,’ replied Evelyn, shaking her head at her father’s foolishness. ‘I can’t see him.’ Evelyn walked around the room holding her candle up to golden statues.

‘Yes, yes, good point.’ Carnarvon turned and started looking around the chamber. There was no sign of a coffin or sarcophagus.

‘I think he’s through here.’ Carter was standing in front of a white stone wall with a golden statue of a man either side of it. ‘These statues are guarding something.’

‘Yes, he must be in there,’ said Carnarvon, licking his lips excitedly. ‘Where’s the hammer?’

‘Now, let’s calm down.’ Carter held up his hand. ‘We can’t open a royal tomb without someone from the Department of Antiquities present.’

‘What? Don’t be ridiculous, man! This is my property.’ Carnarvon was obviously upset and desperate to open up the inner chamber.

'Unfortunately the Egyptians don't agree with you, sir,' said Carter. 'They argue that any valuables found in Egypt belong to the Egyptian Government.'

'Nonsense! I've paid a fortune to find this tomb! No one is going to take the treasure from me now.'

'I agree, sir,' said Carter. 'But I don't want to spend the rest of my life in an Egyptian prison.'

Carnarvon thought about it for a while, imagining what life would be like for an elderly English aristocrat in a rough Arab jail. 'I suppose you're right,' he said, finally.

'Can't we just have a quick look, though?' asked Evelyn. 'We could make a small hole in the corner and then cover it back up. We can say that we found it like that, no one would ever know.' She looked from one man to the other.

Carter was even more desperate to see the inner chamber than the other two. He thought about it for a second, weighing his options. This moment was what he had been waiting for; it was the culmination of years of work. Now he would have the chance to see Tutankhamun without officials, journalists and photographers making the moment theirs… not his.

After a minute, he nodded. 'All right,' he said, 'let's have a quick look. But we mustn't touch anything.'

'Yes, yes, no problem,' said Carnarvon, handing Carter the hammer and chisel. 'Let's be quick, Carter.'

Carter did exactly as Evelyn had suggested. He made a small hole, just big enough for them to squeeze through, in the corner of the wall. When he had finished, they stood back for a second to let out the putrid air from inside.

'Who's going first this time?' asked Evelyn.

'You can,' said Carter.

Evelyn immediately dropped down on all fours and climbed through the hole. Carnarvon followed and then Carter. Once inside, they could hardly believe what they saw: the whole chamber was covered in hieroglyphics and paintings; gold statues lined the walls; and there, in the middle of the room, was a coffin.

'Is he in there?' whispered Carnarvon.

'There's only one way to find out,' said Carter. He wiped the sweat from his brow and moved next to the stone coffin. There were more hieroglyphics engraved on the lid. There was a strange silence. Carter could hear his own heart thumping in his chest. He swallowed hard and then slid his fingers under the lid. It was heavy, but with a push, it moved slightly.

'Be careful!' whispered Evelyn.

Carter pushed as hard as he could until a gap about ten centimeters wide appeared. He held his candle closer to the coffin and gasped. A face of solid gold with white eyes stared back at him. It was Tutankhamun's death mask. The Boy King's delicate features glowed in the soft candlelight.

'Sir, have a look at what we've found,' whispered Carter, moving aside so that Carnarvon could see what was inside the coffin.

'My God,' said Carnarvon. He started to smile and then to laugh. 'We've done it! We've actually found him!'

'Yes, sir,' said Carter, wiping a tear from his eye and looking again at the face of Tutankhamun. 'We found him.'

The discovery of Tutamkhamun's tomb was a huge worldwide news story and Howard Carter became famous almost overnight. Most of the treasures that were found in the tomb have stayed in Egypt, including the amazing death mask that was on his mummy, but others are in museums around the world. Tutankhamun's body is still in his tomb in the Valley of the Kings.

The Beach

Part One

It was the first time that Private Thomas Hart had seen the ocean. His home state, Nevada, was landlocked; he'd never even sailed on a lake before. For a moment he took in the rolling waves and the smell of salt in the spray on his face.

'Are you OK, Hart?' Lieutenant Peters gripped the young soldier by the shoulders. Hart shook his head and the sound of the sea was replaced by gunfire and the boat's engine. It was June 6th, 1944, and the Allied Forces were invading France to fight the Nazis.

'Yes, sir!'

'Once the gate drops, I want you to run into the water. Remember, you have to get to the beach!' Lieutenant Peters grabbed Hart's jacket and pulled him close to his face. 'Do not die today, soldier!'

'Yes, sir!' Hart shouted. He could hardly hear himself speak over the thunderous sounds all around him. He looked up at the sky and saw British planes flying towards the beach.

'Hart!' Lieutenant Peters looked Hart straight in the eyes to make sure he understood what he was saying. 'When you get to the beach, turn left and go straight for about one hundred meters. We will meet on the western side of the beach. Remember the pictures I showed you!'

Hart could barely remember anything in the chaos. 'I remember the picture, sir!' he lied.

'Good! Remember, there are Nazi gunners there. Our mission is to destroy them.'

'Yes, sir!'

Lieutenant Peters turned to the next soldier.

Hart looked at his fellow soldiers across the small boat they were in; one was praying, another was vomiting. Hart looked behind him. He could just see the ships that they had left on the small landing craft that they were now in. He looked ahead and could see the beach coming closer and closer. There were flashes of light from gunfire and tracer bullets that zipped between the soldiers scrambling up the beach.

In that second, Hart thought about his hometown, Ruth, Nevada. It was a peaceful town near a copper mine, where Hart had worked before becoming a soldier. He wondered if he would ever see it again.

'The gate is opening soon!' someone shouted. Hart stood up. He closed his eyes and said a silent prayer.

Hart felt something drip from his nose. He looked up at the grey clouds and noticed that it had started to rain. It was a light rain, but it would make getting to the beach that much harder. The recruits had found out during training in England that running through water was extremely slow and energy-sapping. A B-17 bomber flew overhead. The noise from its engines vibrated his chest. 'Almost there!' Lieutenant Peters yelled above the noise.

Hart bent forward and checked the shoelaces on his combat boots. He ran his hand along the pistol attached to his thigh and touched the C-4 explosive in his backpack. A huge fountain of water sprayed into the boat, drenching the soldiers in cold seawater.

'What was that?' someone cried.

'It was a water mine!' Lieutenant Peters shouted. 'We're lucky it wasn't right under us. Remember, boys, the Nazis have an advantage over us! Get to the beach as quickly as possible… you don't want to get stuck in the water! You don't…'

Hart couldn't hear what else Peters was saying over the tremendous noise from the battle on the beach. He watched the lieutenant's silent lips as they moved. Suddenly, Lieutenant Peters gave the signal to open the gate. It dropped and bullets instantly started flying all around them.

'Go! Go! Go! Go!' the lieutenant cried, pushing the men out of the boat and into the water.

Bullets scattered into the boat. Soldiers fell all around Hart as he made his way to the gate. He felt a hand on his shoulder, then Lieutenant Peters pushed him into the cold sea and jumped in after him.

Water filled the young soldier's lungs. He went up for air and heard more bullets hitting the water around his head. He kicked his legs, found solid ground and stood up. He was relieved that the weight of his pack was no longer dragging him beneath the waves. He needed to get onto the beach; at least he'd be able to run once he got there.

Hart waded forward as quickly as he could. Soldiers were being killed all around him. Some were hit by bullets, others were simply drowning under the weight of their equipment. He looked behind him and saw Lieutenant Peters helping soldiers as they came out of the boat. Hart looked left; the water was filled with other American boats and soldiers who were trying to get to the beach before getting shot. Some of them fell into the water once bullets hit them; others helped their friends along. A few were swimming away from the shore, back towards the boats.

He turned and faced the beach. He was just a few meters from the shore now.

Part Two

Thomas Hart had only learned to swim about eight years ago, when he was ten years old. His mom had forced him to take a swimming class at the local pool. At the time, he had hated swimming lessons, but he was glad now that he had given up those Saturday mornings.

Thunder rumbled in the sky. A bullet hissed past him and struck a soldier in the chest. The man fell backwards into the water. Even with the darkness of the clouds, the water was starting to turn red with blood.

Two meters to shore. More explosions and bullets. More death.

He was going to reach the beach. He was moving faster every moment, his legs gaining power as the water became shallower. He took his first step onto the sand on Omaha Beach. He wanted to scream out, 'I survived!', but he knew that was far from certain; there were even more bodies on the beach than in the sea behind him.

Another B-17 bomber dropped bombs onto the beach about four hundred meters away. Hart dived behind a metal object to protect himself. The Nazis had lined the beach with Czech hedgehogs – large metal objects with spikes on all sides. They made it practically impossible for tanks to drive onto the beach.

Hart took a deep breath and tried to calm his nerves. He knew that if he panicked, he was as good as dead. He needed to head west on the beach to rally with the troops there, but heading west would be difficult. Thunder cracked in the sky. Bullets hit the hedgehogs, creating a loud, dinging sound. Hart spotted Lieutenant Peters running towards him.

'Lieutenant!' he cried out.

A bullet whizzed past Hart's ear and Peters fell to the ground.

'Lieutenant!' Hart fired in the direction of the enemy from behind the hedgehog. He kept shooting until he felt a hand grab hold of his ankle. He looked down to see Peters staring up at him.

'Are you hit, sir?' Hart leaned down and pulled the lieutenant behind the metal hedgehog.

'I'm fine, Hart!'

'I thought you were dead! I saw the bullet…'

'It grazed me.' The lieutenant showed him a three inch streak of blood on his shoulder. 'I'll be fine. We need to get to the western point and clear the way there. We have tanks planning to come that way in the next two hours. We have to move now, but one at a time. Do not move in a pack! It makes us too easy to hit.'

More soldiers had now gathered around them. The group started moving west, providing cover for each other.

Lieutenant Peters led the way, knowing that some of the men were very inexperienced. A huge Nazi tank positioned on a cliff began firing down at them. The tanks shells hit the beach, and sand exploded all around them.

'We have to stop that tank!' Hart screamed, firing in the tank's direction.

'Keep moving, Hart!' Peters shouted. 'You won't do any damage from this distance!'

They kept moving along the beach in single file, crouching and ducking to avoid the bullets. They suddenly stopped. 'Landmines!' one of the soldiers, Kimble, called out.

Kimble and another man, Turner, took ropes out of their backpacks. While Lieutenant Peters and his men provided fire cover, the two soldiers dragged the ropes through the sand. 'All clear!' Turner shouted, waving the soldiers on.

They continued forward to the western meeting point. Hart was acting solely on instinct now. He ducked as he ran, firing when he had a chance. His training had helped, but it could never have prepared him for this. The sky opened up and rays of light came down to the beach. There was something very beautiful about it, something very different from the violence taking place around him.

'Quit daydreaming and start shooting!' Peters said to Hart. They were behind another hedgehog now, close to the meeting point.

'Up ahead!' The lieutenant pointed at a small shack about twenty meters away. Two Nazi soldiers were shooting down at the beach using a large machine gun. The bullets never seemed to stop, and the only way to get to the meeting point was to pass this shack.

'Do you have your C-4?' Peters asked Hart.

'Yes, sir!'

C-4 was a type of powerful explosive. Everyone in Hart's division had a C-4 pack with them. This allowed them to blow up obstacles.

'Good, we will provide you with fire cover. I want you to crawl over there and blow the shack up.'

'Crawl over there?' The blood drained from Hart's face.

'You're the best I've got when it comes to explosives,' the lieutenant said. 'Just remember your training. We won't let them get you!'

'Yes, sir!'

Part Three

'Go! Go!' the lieutenant shouted.

Hart started crawling towards the small shack. He could see the two German soldiers inside, loading bullets into the machine gun. One pointed down at the beach, and the gun started firing. Hart pressed his body even closer to the sand. He was sure he was going to die at that moment, positive that the bullets would hit him. Peters and the others started firing at the shack, distracting the gunners away from Hart.

Hart knew that it was now or never. He was five meters away from the left side of the shack. He crawled as quickly as he could through the wet sand. His muscles were aching and his eyes were stinging from the salt and grit. He was close enough now to hear the Nazi soldiers speaking in German. They hadn't noticed his progress up the beach. They continued firing their machine gun at Peters and the rest of the group.

Hart buried the C-4 pack under the sand and pressed it against the bottom of the shack. He looked back at Peters, but the lieutenant was too busy directing the soldiers to notice that Hart had completed his mission. He started to crawl away from the shack, carrying with him a thin wire that he would use to detonate the explosive.

He had got just a few meters away when bullets started hitting the beach all around him, throwing clouds of sand in the air and into his eyes. Hart crawled even faster now, not knowing where the bullets were coming from. A bullet struck him in the leg. The pain shot through his body, and he rolled onto his side. He looked back at the Nazi gunners, trying to judge how far away he was from the shack. His leg throbbed; the pain was overwhelming.

More bullets started hitting the sand around him. There wasn't anything else he could do. He pressed the button that triggered the C-4 explosive. The small shack exploded with an ear-splitting boom, sending sharp pieces of wood and metal into the air.

Hart closed his eyes.

He was back in Nevada now, eating dinner with his family. His brother, Cody, was there, and their grandmother and their aunt. They were eating steak, green beans and mashed potatoes. Music was playing on the old record player in the living room. Life was beautiful again.

'Where am I?' Hart asked his brother.

'You're here,' Cody said, looking confused.

'Here? Where's here?'

'Home…' his brother laughed at the strange question.

Hart heard the sound of bullets and explosions again. He opened his eyes. He was back in Normandy, back on that wretched beach.

'Hart! Wake up!' Lieutenant Peters slapped his face. 'Medic!' he cried. 'We have a man down!'

'Am I alive?' Hart asked.

'Yes, Hart… but you've lost your leg, so we need you out of here.'

Hart reached down to touch his leg. There was nothing there. 'What happened to it?' he asked.

Lieutenant Peters looked the young soldier in the eye. 'Everything will be OK, son. Good work, Hart. You did well.'

Peters stood up and started shouting orders to the rest of the group. Hart turned his head and watched as his fellow soldiers made their way up the beach towards the terrible guns. He prayed that this day would end well for them. He prayed for victory.

November 22nd, 1963

8.38am. In Fort Worth, Texas, John Fitzgerald Kennedy, the 35th President of the United States of America, meets his appointments secretary, Kenneth O'Donnell, to discuss the day ahead. The President is in high spirits and looking forward to the visit to Dallas later that day.

8.37am. In Dallas, Abraham Zapruder finishes his breakfast and looks out of the window. Zapruder is a Democrat and a huge fan of President Kennedy. He is also a keen amateur photographer and home movie maker. Zapruder is looking forward to getting some footage of the President later, but it looks as if the rain is here to stay.

8.42am. Nurse Sally Hudson arrives at Parklands Memorial Hospital on the outskirts of Dallas, ready to start her shift in the emergency room. It's a Friday like any other. Sally greets her colleagues as she makes her way down to the ER. She is disappointed that she won't be able to go and see the President later, but that is the life of a nurse – her job and her patients must always come first.

9.05am. Lee Harvey Oswald wakes a little later than usual. He had trouble sleeping the night before but eventually dropped off at about 4am. He takes a shower and then cleans his rifle. Everything seems as it should be. He cooks some eggs and bacon for himself and then turns on the TV. The news is showing images of the crowd at Dallas Love Field airport waiting for the arrival of the President. Oswald smiles and turns off the TV.

9.31am. Abraham Zapruder arrives at Jennifer Juniors, the clothing company that he founded in 1948. On arrival, he is greeted by his young assistant, Nick Mason. Mason is extremely excited about the President's visit as the Jennifer Juniors factory is just minutes from Dealey Plaza, where the President's motorcade will pass. Mason asks Zapruder where his 8mm Bell and Howell camcorder is and is shocked to hear that Zapruder has left it at home due to the bad weather. Mason insists that Zapruder go home and get the camera. The forecast is for sunshine and clear skies later.

10.37am. Lee Harvey Oswald puts his rifle, a revolver and some extra ammunition in a bag and puts it over his shoulder. He feels calm and relaxed. Oswald's Russian wife, Marina, and their baby daughter are still sleeping. The couple met in Moscow when Oswald had defected to the Soviet Union, but they are now living permanently back in the United States. He writes a note for his wife and leaves it on the sideboard. It is a simple note telling her how much he loves her and that he will see her after he finishes work that evening. Oswald leaves the house and starts walking towards the Texas School Book Depository Building on Dealey Plaza, where he started working a month before.

10.48am. Nurse Sally Hudson is watching the news in the nurses' break room at Parklands Hospital. She and the other nurses talk about how disappointed they are that they won't get to see the President.

10.57am. Aboard Air Force One, the President's private plane, O'Donnell tells Kennedy of the exact route that they will take through Dallas. The President likes to feel close to the people, even though it makes the Secret Service and all his advisors extremely nervous. They would prefer him to make a speech and then get somewhere more secure, but the President insists on the drive through Dallas so that he can wave to the crowds. The route they have chosen gives the President maximum exposure to the crowd. This also makes it highly dangerous. As it has stopped raining, Kennedy asks that the roof of the convertible car be down while they drive through the city.

11.01am. Abraham Zapruder arrives back at Jennifer Juniors with his camera. Nick Mason, his assistant, is delighted; he is also an amateur film maker and is looking forward to shooting some footage of the day using Zapruder's camera. The two men go outside and start looking for a good vantage point from which to film the motorcade as it passes.

11.17am. Air Force One lands at Love Field. The President and his beautiful wife, Jackie, leave the aircraft and wave to the thousands of Texans who have gathered to welcome their leader to their city. It's a warm day. The President is feeling happy and relaxed. He waves to the crowd and poses for more pictures. The President then gets into a Lincoln Convertible for the drive through Dallas.

11.24am. Lee Harvey Oswald arrives at the Texas School Book Depository Building on the corner of Houston Street and Elm Street. The building overlooks the route that the presidential motorcade will take. Oswald found out about the planned route in October and immediately applied for a job there. Oswald greets some of his co-workers as he climbs the stairs to the sixth floor.

11.44am. John F Kennedy turns to his wife and comments on the size of the crowds lining the streets as their motorcade makes its way slowly from Love Field towards Dallas. There are six people in the President's Lincoln Convertible: the President; his wife, Jackie; the Governor of Texas, John Connally and his wife, Nellie; the driver, Bill Greer; and a Secret Service agent named Roy Kellerman.

11.56am. Nurse Sally Hudson is surprised at how quiet the ER is. Midday on a weekday is usually a busy time, mostly traffic accidents, but so many people are off work and so many roads are closed that things are quiet for the medical staff at Parklands Hospital.

12.01pm. Abraham Zapruder and Nick Mason have found an excellent place to watch the motorcade from. They are on a grassy hill overlooking Elm Street. They should be able to get some great footage of the President from there.

12.14pm. Lee Harvey Oswald wipes his hands on his pants and takes a deep breath. Suddenly, one of his colleagues, John Frazier, enters the room and asks Oswald what he's doing on the sixth floor; Oswald usually works on the third floor. Oswald explains that he just wants to catch a glimpse of the President as he passes by on Elm Street six floors below. Frazier seems satisfied and leaves. As soon as his colleague has gone, Oswald removes his rifle from the bag and puts it on the floor by the window. He takes six bullets from the bag and loads them into the gun. Oswald trained as a marine before he defected to the Soviet Union. He knows how to handle a rifle.

12.16pm. Abraham Zapruder films the crowd. Thousands of people have come to wave to the President and his wife, Jackie. Kennedy is one of the youngest Presidents in the country's history, and the most popular President America has had since the war. Zapruder, and millions like him, believe that this young president will lead America to a bright and prosperous future.

12.18pm. Oswald cleans the scope of his rifle and checks that it is in focus. He adjusts the scope slightly and leans the gun against the wall next to the window. He is ready.

12.23pm. The President's Lincoln Convertible turns off Houston Street onto Elm Street in Dealey Plaza. They pass the Texas School Depository Building.

12.24pm. Abraham Zapruder films the motorcade as it comes down Elm Street towards him.

12.26pm. Sally Hudson and the other nurses are having lunch. They watch the news on a small black and white TV in the cafeteria at Parklands Hospital, but there is no live footage being broadcast.

12.28pm. Oswald can now see the President. He can't fire yet because there is a tree obscuring his sight, making the shot impossible. He must wait one more minute.

12.29pm. Nellie Connally turns and says something to the President. Kennedy leans forward slightly to reply.

Lee Harvey Oswald fires his first shot. He misses. The bullet hits the road.

Abraham Zapruder hears a loud crack and immediately turns towards the School Depository Building. His camera, though, is still pointing at the President.

Oswald fires his second shot.

President Kennedy is hit in the neck. The bullet passes through his throat and strikes Governor Connally in the back.

Jackie Kennedy, realizing something is wrong, turns to her husband, who is clutching his throat.

Oswald fires his third and final shot. The bullet enters the back of Kennedy's head and exits through the front, leaving a ten centimeter hole in the President's skull.

12.30pm. Jackie Kennedy panics and starts climbing towards the back of the car but Secret Service agents instruct her to sit down. The driver, Bill Greer, seeing that the President has been shot, accelerates out of Dealey Plaza.

12.31pm. Abraham Zapruder cannot believe what he has seen… and filmed. He and Nick Mason drop down to the grass and cover their heads. The crowd is panicking. Many fear a massacre, but no more shots are fired.

12.36pm. Sally Hudson and the rest of the staff in the cafeteria finish their lunch. There is no news of the shooting on TV yet. Suddenly a doctor comes in and tells everyone to get back to the Emergency Room. The President is coming in with a serious head wound.

12.39pm. Lee Harvey Oswald leaves the Texas School Depository Building. He has left the rifle by the window on the sixth floor, but he still has the revolver in his bag. He starts to walk home.

12.43pm. Officer J D Tipit of the Dallas Police gets a call from police headquarters that the President has been shot. The shooter has not been apprehended. Tipit, and every other officer, is told to look for anyone acting suspiciously.

12.48pm. Kennedy arrives at Parklands Hospital in the Lincoln Convertible. Sally Hudson helps to get the President to Trauma Room One, where doctors immediately give him oxygen and attempt resuscitation, but it is obviously too late.

1.00pm. President John F Kennedy is pronounced dead.

1.15pm. Lee Harvey Oswald knows that the rifle will be discovered soon and that the police will be looking for him. He takes backstreets on his way home, trying to avoid the public and any police officers.

1.20pm. A police officer asks Abraham Zapruder what he saw. Zapruder gives his witness statement and also tells the police officer that he may have it all on film. The police officer takes Zapruder's camera so that the film can be examined.

1.23pm. Lee Harvey Oswald walks through residential Dallas. He tries to act as normally as possible to avoid arousing suspicion.

1.28pm. Nurse Sally Hudson watches as the black bag is zipped up around the face of the dead President Kennedy. She starts to cry.

1.30pm. Officer J D Tipit of the Dallas Police is driving through the Oak Field area of Dallas. Everything seems normal.

1.32pm. Lee Harvey Oswald enters Oak Field. He keeps to the shadows and moves quickly. He is almost home.

1.34pm. Tipit notices a man walking in the shadows of the trees about one hundred meters ahead of him. He follows slowly.

1.35pm. John F Kennedy's body is placed in a casket and taken to an ambulance to be driven to Air Force One at Love Field.

1.36pm. Vice-President Lyndon B Johnson's plane arrives at Love Field.

1.37pm. Officer Tipit stops his patrol car and asks the man his name and where he is going. Lee Harvey Oswald comes out of the shadows of the trees and shoots the policeman four times. Tipit dies instantly.

1.42pm. Sally Hudson and other members of the medical team that treated the President are interviewed by the Secret Service.

1.43pm. Lee Harvey Oswald enters a local movie theater without paying. The ticket clerk, suspecting that something is wrong, stops a passing patrol car.

1.44pm. Vice-President Lyndon B Johnson is taken aboard Air Force One.

1.45pm. Two officers enter the movie theater. They have now heard about the shooting of Officer Tipit and suspect that the man in the cinema may be the man who shot President Kennedy.

Oswald hides in the gloom of the movie theater. There are just two people inside.

The officers spot Oswald in the shadows of the auditorium and move either side of him.

Oswald can see one of the officers, but he has not noticed the other one approaching from his left. He has only two bullets left in his revolver so he must use them wisely.

The officer on Oswald's right moves closer.

Oswald pulls out his revolver and prepares to fire.

The policeman on Oswald's left suddenly appears out of the dark and hits Oswald on the arm, making him drop his weapon.

The two officers disarm and arrest Lee Harvey Oswald of the shooting of Officer J D Tipit and the suspected shooting of President John F Kennedy.

2.00pm. Vice-President Lyndon B Johnson is sworn in as the 36th President of the United States aboard Air Force One. Jackie Kennedy, still in blood-stained clothes, stands beside him. The body of her husband is in a casket at the back of the plane.

The Divided City

Part One

People thought it was impossible. The Russians, under the leadership of Nikolai Krushev, had decided to build a wall through the city of Berlin. It seemed like an impossible task. How could they build a forty-three kilometer wall through a sprawling European city? Berlin had stood for eight hundred years. Families lived on the east and the west side. The people didn't want the wall, but they didn't have a choice.

Early in the morning on August 13th, 1961, the Russian military began building the wall that would divide the city. They moved quickly, rolling out barbed wire and delivering bricks. My father, who owned a small store on the western side of the wall, sighed. 'They really are serious,' he said, after he returned from the construction site.

'What are they doing?' Martin, my younger brother, asked.

'They are building a wall!'

'To divide the city?' our mother asked. She was in an apron, arranging cabbages on a wooden crate.

'Can I see?'

'Sure, Erich,' my father said. 'But if you are going out, please stop by Mr Honecker's shop and see if he has received his shipment of apples.'

'OK!' I ran out of the shop, down the block, and turned the corner. I stopped when I saw a group of armed soldiers patrolling the construction site. Behind them, Germans and Russians were busy constructing the wall.

I shoved my hands in my pockets and pretended not to stare. A crowd had gathered on the western side of the new wall. A few journalists were with the crowd, taking pictures. There were also some American soldiers with weapons standing near the construction site. A riot would start later, but I would be safe inside my home by then.

Soldiers wearing brown uniforms were busy surveying the start of the new wall. I tried to think of where exactly the wall was being built. It seemed as if it would come straight down the street. I looked to my right, to the place where my best friend Konrad lived. Konrad and I had gone to elementary school together. We met almost every day to play and to explore the city. Sometimes, he would help us around the shop. My mother liked to call him her 'third son.' We were inseparable, but things were about to get a lot more difficult.

The Russians were building the wall between Konrad's home and the street. Konrad's home would be on the eastern side of the city and ours would be on the western side. They hadn't started construction yet, but they had put barbed wire on the ground. I ran through an opening in the barbed wire and over to his house.

'Konrad!' I shouted, seeing that his window was open.

He came to the window. 'Erich!' His father appeared behind him.

'They're building a wall,' I said, pointing at the barbed wire.

'I know!'

Both of us were children at the time and hadn't quite realized what this wall would do to our friendship.

'When did they start?' I asked.

'Early in the morning! My dad has to help them later...' he started to say.

'That's enough, Konrad,' his father said, putting a hand on his son's shoulder.

'Can you come out and play?' I called up to him.

A soldier appeared nearby. He seemed to be talking to one of his commanders. They looked over at me; the commander was pointing at the hole in the barbed wire that I had run through.

'Go home, Erich,' Konrad's father said. 'Now! It's dangerous here.'

'But…'

'Now!'

I'd never heard Konrad's father raise his voice. Like any kid who has been scolded by an adult, I turned and ran as quickly as I could, back through the hole in barbed wire and to the western side of the street. I didn't know at the time, but it would be the last time I saw Konrad for many years.

Part Two

It took them a little over a month to build the wall separating East and West Berlin. Many people didn't know what to do. Some of my relatives who lived in East Berlin were able to escape before the wall was finished. Others weren't so lucky. Checkpoint Charlie was set up near my home. The checkpoint allowed people to legally cross from East Berlin to West Berlin, but only if they had the right documents.

My father didn't think that building the Berlin Wall was a good idea at all. 'They can't divide an entire city!' he would say every morning as he read the newspaper. 'People will do anything to get to the other side. They will climb over the wall or build tunnels. The people of Berlin can't be separated from each other!'

He was right about the tunnels. As soon as the wall was finished, East Berliners began digging tunnels under the wall. The tunnels usually started in the basement of someone's house. They had to be careful because of the sewers. They also had to know where the tunnel would come up on the western side of the city. Eventually, Russian soldiers began using listening equipment. They would listen to the walls, and if they heard digging, they would arrest the people making the tunnel.

However, my father was wrong about people climbing the wall. It was foolish to climb the wall because of all the barbed wire. Also, there were watchtowers along the wall, making it very difficult to cross. Several East Berliners were shot trying to climb the wall. This made matters very complicated because the Americans soldiers didn't know what to do if they saw someone crossing the wall, and the Russian soldiers didn't want to get the person down from the wall, because they thought the Americans would shoot.

Things really got bad in October. I noticed some people running towards Checkpoint Charlie while I was on my way to school one day.

'Come on, Martin!' I said to my little brother. 'Let's go and see what's happening!'

'But Erich,' he cried, 'we need to get to school!'

'This will be more interesting than school…'

We ran several blocks, dodging people on their way to work and shop owners opening up their shops. We arrived near Checkpoint Charlie and saw that a large crowd had formed.

'Look!' Martin said, pointing at a US airplane flying overhead. It was very big; it sounded like some sort of monster.

'Come on,' I said, grabbing his hand. We pushed our way through the crowd. It was easy to do this because we were smaller than the adults. We stopped once we saw about thirty US tanks with their guns aimed at the other side of Checkpoint Charlie. On the East side, about thirty Russian tanks' guns were aimed directly at us.

'It's a standoff!' I said.

A man in a grey suit put his hand on my shoulder. 'Do your parents know you're here?'

I didn't answer. Instead, I grabbed my younger brother's hand and went deeper into the crowd. We stopped again once we'd lost the man.

'Are they going to fight?' my brother asked. He had a few toy tanks and sometimes played with them in our living room.

'I don't know,' I said, recognizing the severity of the situation. There was a chill in the air; people were afraid of what would happen next. After about twenty minutes, the Russian tanks started to back up.

'They're turning back!' I said.

The crowd began to cheer. It was a small victory for West Berlin, but the problems still remained. A giant wall divided the city, and Konrad, my best friend, lived on the other side of the wall.

Part Three

In 1979, eighteen years after the Berlin Wall was built, something miraculous happened. I was managing my father's business at the time. We had been prosperous in West Berlin and had opened ten other grocery stores across the city.

I preferred to work at the grocery store that was near Checkpoint Charlie. I hadn't heard from my best friend, Konrad, in eighteen years, but part of me believed I would see him one day. It was a foolish belief. For all I knew, he had started a family in East Berlin and had completely forgotten about me. Still, I looked out of the window of the shop from time to time, expecting to see him.

It was a cool day, slightly breezy and depressing. The grey days in Berlin always felt depressing to me. At around ten, I decided to go for a stroll. I told my dad, who was in the back room going over our finances, that I was popping out. He didn't mind watching the shop; he knew that I worked better when I had a clear mind.

I decided to walk on the street opposite the wall. This wasn't the usual path that I took, I usually walked in the alleys behind Mauer Street. As I walked along, I noticed something red floating in the air above the wall.

I started running, getting as close to the wall as I could. Then, a hot air balloon passed over me. I looked up just in time to see a sniper's bullet hit the balloon.

I couldn't see how many people were in the balloon, all I could see was the bottom of the basket, which was now falling onto the western side of the wall. A man walking next to the wall looked over at me. Both of us knew what needed to be done—we had to help the people that were in the balloon.

Another sniper bullet hit the top of the basket. The balloon was floating back over to the other side of the wall. I could hear the scream of a child, a young girl, inside the balloon's basket. 'Papa!' she cried.

Snap!

One of the ropes that held the balloon to the basket broke. Then another broke. Only two ropes, one at each corner of the basket, were stopping the people from falling.

'What should we do?' the guy next to me asked, but I had already sprung into action.

I moved towards the street, where cars had stopped and people were getting out. I noticed the rope hanging from the basket. Air was hissing out of the balloon and if I didn't do something soon, the basket would spill into the street. Luckily, I grabbed the rope just in time.

I started running, holding the rope. This straightened out the basket. I could hear the girl crying inside and could now see her father peeking over the sides at the street below. The Russian soldiers wouldn't dare shoot bullets over the wall, but their guns were still pointed at the balloon.

Another hand grabbed part of the rope. It was the man from earlier who had first seen the hot air balloon with me. We worked as quickly as we could to safely bring the hot air balloon to the ground. Inside the basket was a family of four: a father, a mother, a young girl and a baby. We had saved their entire family.

Part Four

By the time 1989 came around, I was married and had two children. I was running my father's business alone now as my father had retired. There was talk of the Berlin Wall coming down, but people my age didn't believe it. We had lived with the wall nearly all our lives. That was why I was so surprised by what happened in the autumn of that year.

Tensions were already high; many East Berliners had escaped to West Berlin through Hungary. On November 9th, the situation in East Berlin had become too difficult to control. It was announced that night on the news that the checkpoints would be opened.

A funny thing happened next. Naturally, some people lined up at the checkpoints waiting to move peacefully from east to west. However, the vast majority of Berliners from both sides of the wall took to the wall with all sorts of construction equipment; hammers, picks and shovels were used to break down the wall.

I can still remember the excitement in the air. I had a pick in my hand and had been taking down parts of the wall all night. It was exhilarating to think that such a big part of my life, this ugly wall, would disappear. By instinct, I worked on the piece of the wall that had separated the street from my best friend Konrad's old apartment. It had been almost thirty years since we had last seen each other, but I had a feeling that if I could find him anywhere, it would be there.

The crowd worked into the night dismantling the wall. Some people cried and others cheered. I had never witnessed so much pure emotion in my life. I felt like the destruction of that wall was the destruction of everything bad in this world. At around two in the morning, I heard someone call my name from the other side of the wall. I pushed my way to the front of the crowd and saw Konrad.

'I thought that was you!' he said, running to hug me. He had gained weight and had lost most of his hair. He still had the same clever eyes and sharp nose he had when we were children. 'You look well fed!' he said, punching me in the stomach.

'Yes!' I was overwhelmed with emotion. I had no idea what to say to him, luckily he was more talkative.

'How have you been, Erich?' he asked, hugging me again. 'I can't believe it has been so long…'

'I've been well,' I finally said.

We hugged one more time and we turned back to the crumbling wall. We worked together for the rest of the night, taking down as much of the Berlin Wall as we could. It was the dawn of a new age for our friendship, for our city and for the entire country of Germany.

The Berlin Wall stood from August 13th, 1961 until November 9th, 1989. It was forty-three kilometers long and nearly four meters high. There were over three hundred watchtowers along the wall and at least 136 people died trying to cross it. These days, the Berlin Wall is remembered as both a physical structure and as a symbol of the Cold War, which took place between Western and Soviet powers from 1947-1991.

The Aftermath

Part One

A small boat steered by a thin black man entered the Lower Ninth Ward. It was the dead of night. The water covering the neigborhood was more than three meters high. Hurricane Katrina had destroyed the city of New Orleans. Now, people were stranded, hungry and desperate. The man used a long stick to guide his boat through the flood waters. He was holding a flashlight in his hand, and slowly chewed on a piece of gum.

The man pressed his stick against a street sign and stopped his boat. He looked up at the sign and shook his head. He hadn't even recognized his own street, the street that he'd grown up on and lived on all of his life. The man's house was at the end of this street, Walnut Street it was called, but it would take some time before he got there.

'I can see you.'

The man in the boat followed the sound to the roof of a house. He turned his flashlight towards the voice. 'I can't see you,' he called back. He spat his gum into the gloomy water and waited for a response.

'Name?' the voice asked.

'My name is Amos... Amos Washington.'

'I don't know that name.' Amos could tell that it was a younger man, younger than him anyway.

'Don't play games with me, son,' Amos said, peering up through the darkness. 'I've lived on this street my whole life. I grew up playing in the playground over on Marcy and I went to school at…'

'I've never heard of you,' the voice interrupted him. The flood water covering the neighborhood was high and as black as oil. The moon was blocked by a dark cloud. Amos heard the sound of a shotgun being loaded.

'Now wait a minute,' Amos said. 'Put your gun away, son. I'm not here to steal anything. I'm just trying to go home. I need to find…'

'What do you need to find?' the younger man asked.

'I'm trying to find my dog,' Amos said.

His dog, Miles, was all Amos had. His wife had died fifteen years ago and they never had children. The house and his dog were the only things left that he cared about... and now the house was under water.

'What does your dog look like?' the voice asked.

'He has white fur, one blue eye and one brown eye. Have you seen him?'

'Nope,' the voice called down to him.

Amos aimed his flashlight in the direction of the man's voice. He couldn't see the man's face, but he could see a portion of his shadow.

'How long have you been up there?' Amos tried to keep his tone friendly. He knew that people were terrified and that made them jumpy.

'Three days now,' the voice from the rooftop said.

'Family?' Silence. 'Sorry to hear that,' Amos said.

'It isn't your fault. The hurricane…' The man's voice changed. Amos sensed that he was about to cry. 'The hurricane destroyed everything.'

'Yes, she did,' Amos said. He remembered the way Hurricane Katrina had swept through New Orleans like an angry bull, destroying everything in its path. The winds were powerful enough to blow down houses. The rain was strong enough to collapse roofs. Amos saw cars floating down the street and trees snapped in half. He saw bodies floating among the clothes and furniture. It was terrible. Truly awful.

'I've been up here for three days…' the voice called down to him. 'Three long days.'

'Do you want to come down?' Amos asked.

'I'm protecting my house…'

'Do you have any food?'

'Why?' the voice asked.

'Don't worry, I don't want any of your food,' Amos said, hearing the suspicion in the man's voice. 'I have some extra food here in my boat, though.'

'Where are you staying?'

'I'm staying on a friend's floor over on North Rampart Street.'

'How bad was the flood over there?' the voice asked.

'Not as bad as here.' Amos shook his head. 'Look, mister, I need to search for Miles. You can help me if you want.'

'Will you bring me back to my house after?'

'Of course I will,' Amos promised. 'What's your name, son?'

'My name is Jordan,' the man said as he climbed down from the roof.

Part Two

Jordan was twice the size of Amos. He was wearing a New Orleans Saints baseball cap. There was a shotgun in his hand, and a backpack on his back. Amos shone his light into the boat as Jordan got in.

'So, which one is your house?' Jordan asked.

'221 Walnut Street. It's a little yellow house with a small oak tree near the driveway.' Amos frowned. 'Well, it used to have a little oak tree. It's probably gone now.'

'A little yellow house…' Jordan said. 'Two stories, right?'

'That's the one.'

'I know that house!' Jordan said.

'That's where I want to search for Miles. I hope he's still there.' Amos used his stick to push the boat further down the street. The moon reflected off the thick water.

Amos steered the boat deeper into the neighborhood. Suddenly, he felt something scrape against the bottom of the boat. There was a loud sound in the water. The boat moved forward and Jordan almost fell overboard. He stopped himself just in time, but wasn't able to save his shotgun. It hit the water and sank into the blackness.

'My shotgun!' Jordan said.

The boat was stuck now, as if something were holding it in place.

‘What could that be?’ Amos asked, dipping his stick into the water. “We’re stuck on something.’

‘My shotgun!’ Jordan said, reaching his arms into the water. His bodyweight moved the boat to the left.

‘I think it’s the top of a car,’ Amos said, hitting his stick against the object in the water. The boat started to tilt as Jordan reached further into the water for his shotgun.

‘You’re going to tip the boat over if you’re not careful, son,’ Amos said calmly.

‘But I dropped my gun…’ Jordan sat down in the boat.

‘You can worry about that later. I need your help right now.’ Amos shone his light into the water. ‘You’re much stronger than I am. Do you think you can reach into the water and push the boat off the top of this car?’

‘All right, All right,’ Jordan said, still cursing under his breath about his shotgun. Jordan reached his hands into the murky water. The water was cold and dark. He imagined sharp-toothed creatures swimming in the thick, black water, and pulled his hands out.

‘Are you scared?’ Amos asked him.

‘No, I’ve just been on my roof for too long.’ Jordan gathered some courage and plunged his hands back in the water. He took a deep breath, and pushed the boat off the top of the car. The boat moved forward. The two men continued down Walnut Street in the boat, towards Amos’s house.

‘What do you do?’ Jordan asked.

‘Well, I’m retired now. I used to work for the New Orleans water treatment plant.’

'Was it a difficult job?'

'It wasn't so bad,' Amos said. 'You?'

'I was, I mean, I am a truck driver. I've been driving the same route between Louisiana, Texas, Oklahoma and Kansas for seven years now.'

'Have you ever found a different route?'

Jordan smiled. 'Nope, but I guess I should now.'

Both men laughed. The tragedy that surrounded them escaped the small boat for a moment. But their laughter suddenly turned to fear as both men heard gunshots.

Bang! Bang! Bang!

'Turn off your flashlight,' Jordan whispered, 'or they'll hit us!'

Amos flicked off his flashlight. The two men lay next to each other in the boat. They drifted into a street sign and stopped.

'What do we do now?' Jordan whispered.

'Be patient for a moment...' Amos said. Amos was a war veteran. This wasn't the first time someone had shot at him.

'Do you think they saw us?' Jordan asked. He was close enough to Amos to feel his hot breath on his face.

'I don't know, but they aren't shining a flashlight on the boat yet. I think they heard us laughing. We should be quieter.'

'I wish I had my shotgun...'

'Don't worry. I brought something along just in case.'

Jordan looked down as moonlight reflected off the silver handle of the pistol that was tucked into Amos's pants.

'You have a gun?'

'Yes, I do,' Amos whispered, 'but I really don't want to use it.'

Part Three

There was a lot of looting in New Orleans after Hurricane Katrina. The people that stayed in their houses wanted to protect their belongings. They put wood over their windows and they painted warning signs on their doors. They also protected their homes with guns. Sometimes it was difficult to tell the difference between a thief and a person searching for their family, or in Amos's case, a person searching for his dog.

'Are you going to shoot at them?' Jordan asked.

Amos and Jordan were lying down in his boat. The water was still and the night was silent. Amos slowly pulled out his gun.

'I don't want to shoot anybody,' Amos said. 'I just want to find Miles, that's all.'

Both men heard a dog bark in the distance. Amos sat up.

'What is it?' Jordan hissed.

'That's him! That's him! Oh, Miles, not right now,' Amos said. He was suddenly very worried.

'That's him?' Jordan asked.

'It sure is. I know that bark. My house is less than a block away. That's him… we have to get over there. How are we going to get away from here?'

Jordan thought for a moment. ‘You said you had some cans of food, right? Put your gun away, I have an idea.’

‘All right. My backpack is down there, by your feet.’

Jordan used his foot to bring the bag between the two men. He opened the bag and took out a can of food.

‘What are you going to do?’ Amos asked.

‘I’m going to create a distraction. As soon as I throw the can, you use your stick to push the boat away from here. Now where were the gun shots coming from?’

‘I don’t know,’ Amos said.

‘Come on, think. Where did the sound come from? Just one gunman, right?’

‘Right.’ Amos thought for a moment. ‘It was three shots, and he fired from the west.’

‘Good!’

Jordan slowly sat up. He saw a street sign about five meters away and threw the can at the street sign. The can hit the water with a splash. He fell back down into the boat and hid next to Amos. Both men waited to hear gunfire, but nothing happened.

‘Try throwing another can,’ Amos whispered.

Jordan sat up slowly again. He saw the street sign and pictured hitting it with his can. He threw the can, and the can smacked against the street sign.

Bang!

He fell back into the boat. Seconds later, they heard gunfire and bullets hitting the street sign.

‘Now!’ Jordan whispered. ‘Go… go…’

Amos used the stick to push the boat away from the gunfire. The little boat moved forward, out of danger, for the moment at least.

Part Four

As Amos approached his house, he thought about Hurricane Katrina. He remembered the sound of the hurricane and the wind and the rain. He had been at his friend's house when the rain started. He was helping his friend board up his windows. He wanted to go home to get Miles, but his friend wouldn't let him leave and it was a good thing—the hurricane had destroyed most of his neighborhood.

'Miles!' Amos called, as they approached his house. He cupped his hands around his mouth and called again. 'Miles!'

He heard Miles barking from the upstairs window. The bottom part of the window was broken, and Miles stuck his head out.

'Miles!' Amos's heart filled with joy. He aimed his flashlight up at the window. Miles was poking his head out of the bottom of the window. The top of the window was still intact.

'Calm down!' Amos called to his dog. He was afraid he might cut his neck on the glass.

'How are we going to get him out of there?' Jordan asked. The little dog barked excitedly.

Amos thought for a moment. He looked up at where Miles was. The broken window was too small for the dog to crawl through.

'We could try and throw a can at the window…' Amos shook his head. 'But we might hit Miles in the head if we do that.'

'I have an idea,' Jordan said. 'I'll climb up onto the roof. I can reach down from the roof, and carefully break the top part of the window.'

'Good idea,' Amos said. He steered the boat to the back of his house. He could hear Miles barking, and it was making him very nervous.

Jordan was a big man, but he was also very strong. He lifted himself onto the roof and crawled over to the window. The house creaked. Suddenly, Amos heard a loud snap.

'What is it?' he yelled up to Jordan.

There was a loud crack and the sound of wood splitting. Miles was barking madly now.

'Are you OK?' Amos shouted.

'My foot went through the roof,' Jordan finally called down. 'It cut my jeans.'

'Are you bleeding?'

'A little…' Jordan moved and the roof creaked. Miles kept barking.

'All right, I'm coming up there!' Amos said. There was panic in his voice, and he was no longer thinking clearly.

'No! Stay in the boat! If you come up here, the roof will collapse. It's still wet from the hurricane. I can get out of this hole.'

Jordan flattened his arms out. He reached down and pulled his leg out of the hole. His leg hurt, but it wasn't broken. He turned his body on the rooftop and crawled towards the front of the house.

'Steer the boat over to the window, but don't get directly underneath,' Jordan called down to Amos. 'I'm going to break the glass.'

'All right!'

Amos steered the boat around his house and stopped a few feet away from the front window.

'I'm here,' he called up to Jordan. He shone his light on the window. He could see Jordan leaning over the roof. He was trying to pull the glass off the window, but couldn't do it.

'Do you have any cans left?' Jordan asked. 'I need something to break this window.'

'I have two more.' Amos reached into his backpack and waved the can in the air. 'Do you think you can catch it?'

'I can try. Toss it up here.'

Amos threw the food can and Jordan caught it. Miles was at the window now, barking through the hole in the bottom of the window. Jordan reached his hand back and smashed the top of the glass with the can. The glass fell into the cold water below. Seconds later, Miles jumped out of the window.

'Miles!' Amos called out. He saw his dog hit the water and instantly start swimming. 'Good boy!' he said as Miles swam over to him.

Amos reached down and pulled Miles into the boat. 'Are you OK, boy? I missed you so much,' he said, hugging his dog. There was a little blood on the dog's body, but other than that, he was fine. Miles licked his face and Amos laughed. 'I was so worried…'

'Don't forget me!' Jordan called down to him. He started laughing as well.

'I'm coming to get you now…' Amos moved the boat to the side of the house. 'Did you see Miles come flying out of that window? He was like a bullet!'

'I didn't expect him to do that,' Jordan said. 'You might need to change that dog's name to Super-Miles.'

Amos laughed as he steadied the boat. Jordan carefully got in and sat down. Miles jumped into Jordan's lap and licked his face.

'This dog sure is friendly!'

'He's probably hungry too. He's been in there for three days.'

Miles barked.

'How's your leg?' Amos asked Jordan.

'It'll be fine. I have a cut above my knee, but it's not so deep.'

The two men drifted back to Jordan's house. They were quiet this time. Jordan held Miles so he wouldn't bark. The sky was starting to turn blue and the sun was minutes away from appearing on the horizon. They arrived at Jordan's house.

'Well, it's been nice,' Amos said, shaking Jordan's hand. 'Sorry about your gun.'

'It's not your fault.' Jordan glanced down at the water. 'How long do you think it will be before the water goes down?'

Amos shook his head. 'I don't know, but you're welcome to come with me.'

Jordan thought for a moment. He looked up at his house, at the roof he had slept on for the last three nights. 'I should probably stay here,' he finally said.

'Well, then you should take this.'

Amos handed Jordan his pistol. 'Just in case,' Amos said. 'Now don't drop that into the water, because I'll be back to get it later. You sure you don't need anything?'

'No, I'll be fine.' Miles barked and both men laughed.

'Sorry, Miles,' Jordan said. 'You can't stay here.'

Jordan pulled himself onto his roof and looked down at Amos. 'Nice to meet you, neighbor.'

'Nice to meet you too, neighbor,' Amos said, waving.

Jordan watched as Amos and Miles disappeared into the early morning mist.

We hope you enjoyed A Day to Remember.

If you have a moment, please let us know what you think by **reviewing our book on Kindle Books.**

Hassan and Lulu

Book One

By Cooper Baltis

.1.

March 21st, 2003

Thousands of kilos of explosives were dropped on the city of Baghdad. Thunderous booms echoed through the city streets, and fires burned brightly. Bombs and missiles lit up the sky, destroying everything they came in contact with. America's Shock and Awe campaign had begun.

'Brother!' Lulu screamed, running into my bedroom. 'Hassan! Hassan!'

'I hear it too!' I yelled. We listened to more explosions near our home. The explosions seemed close and at the same time, far away, as if they were exploding in a dream. The explosions flashed like lightning across the ceiling and the house shook.

'There's no electricity, Hassan,' she said. 'Where's Dad?'

'I don't know…'

Our father, Raheem Mohammed Mosul, was a chemistry professor at Baghdad University. He usually worked late, especially after our mother had died from cancer. Another bomb shook the room.

'That was loud!' Lulu cried.

No one was expecting an attack at this time. Most people assumed it would take the Americans a while to get here. There were some rumors that American forces were coming towards Baghdad from the south, but many people thought that it was just Western propaganda. No one was ready for what would soon come to pass.

Lulu got into my bed and hugged me. 'It's OK, he'll come,' I told her. 'I know he will.'

'What do we do now?' she asked. A sudden flash had frightened her. I could feel her tiny nails digging into my arm. 'Hassan, I'm scared. Where's Dad?'

'Don't worry, Lulu, he'll come. Let's go outside.'

I put on my sandals and told Lulu to follow me. We walked through our hallway to the front door. 'Don't be scared,' I told her as I opened the door. 'Just stay behind me.'

We both gasped at what we saw outside: the sky lit up every time an American jet fired anti-missile flares, turning the dark sky a blood red color. It was like fireworks, but there was no celebration, only destruction.

I looked down at my little sister. She was holding a blanket our mother had made for her. I hadn't noticed the blanket when she'd burst into my room earlier, but I saw it now. I wanted to hide in the blanket with her. I wanted to avoid the devastation of our city and our country. Everything was about to change.

***

March 22nd, 2003

'Do you think he will come back today?' Lulu asked the next morning while I was frying two eggs for her.

'I don't know when Dad will return.' I looked away from my sister. It had been hard to sleep the previous night because of the bombings. Every time I thought it would finally end, another loud explosion shook the house.

'Where do you think he is?'

'He's probably at the university.'

'Do you think he slept there?' she asked. I brought the fried eggs over to her.

'I don't know, Lulu. Eat your eggs.'

'I want to watch TV.'

'Eat,' I said sternly. 'If we still have electricity later, you can watch TV then.'

We ate in silence, mostly because I didn't want to talk. I didn't know where our father was, and I was worried about the American invasion. It was happening. Before Lulu woke up, I had listened to the radio. American forces would be in Baghdad within two weeks. Marines were coming from southern Iraq with tanks. They hoped to capture our president, Saddam Hussein, by the end of the week.

Lulu finished her food and ran to the kitchen. She stood on a small stool near the sink and washed her plate. 'Let's go outside!'

‘We should just stay in here,’ I said. Lulu was eight years old and I was seventeen. It was my job to look after her.

‘Please, please, please Hassan! We went outside last night and it was OK. I just want to see the city.’

I knew exactly what she meant. We used to climb onto the roof of our house a few years before. From the roof of our house, we could see the entire city of Baghdad.

‘Fine, let’s go.’

‘Yes!’ Lulu jumped down from her stool and ran to find her sandals. My sister was thin with curly hair. She was average height for an eight year old girl, but her skinny arms and legs made her look taller than she really was. She appeared moments later in her sandals.

‘Come on! Don’t forget the chair!’

Lulu and I went around to the back of our house. I set the chair on top of a stack of bricks. I held the chair so that she could climb up onto the roof of our house. She turned and looked down at me from the roof. The sun was very bright. Sweat rolled down my cheek and I wiped it away.

‘Be careful!’ she said.

‘I will. It’s not that high.’ I said. I climbed onto the chair and pulled myself up to the rooftop.

***

Our neighborhood was called Adhamiya, which meant 'Pearl of Rosafa'. Adhamiya was on the eastern side of the Tigris River, near a large highway. Our neighborhood's main attraction was the Abu Hanifa Mosque, which was famous for its tall and beautiful minarets.

'Look!' Lulu said, pointing over at the city of Baghdad. We were about ten kilometres away from the city center.

I took a deep breath to calm my nerves. Black clouds of smoke hung over the city. There were fires burning everywhere. Sometimes, an explosion sent fire and smoke into the air. Part of me wanted to scream and another part of me wanted to hide. My stomach turned over and my heart dropped when I thought that our father was somewhere in that burning hell. I sat down on the roof and pulled my knees to my chest. I didn't want Lulu to see how worried I was.

'Why are the Americans coming?' Lulu asked. She lay down on the roof and crossed her arms behind her head.

'It's complicated.' I thought about what my father had told me, that the Americans were coming for our oil. According to my father, America had convinced the world that they needed to liberate Iraq. They'd always been interested in our oil, and had tried for years to get to it somehow. The fact that Saddam Hussein was a cruel dictator only helped their cause. The Americans couldn't have planned a better scenario for an invasion.

'Tell me…'

'I said it's complicated.' I looked down into her eyes. Suddenly, I heard an earth-shattering sound. Dust blew around our heads.

'What is it?' Lulu screamed. A sudden strong wind bent the trees near our house.

A black helicopter appeared above us. I pulled my sister close and covered her ears. The helicopter hovered above us for a long time, its blades slicing through the air like knives. Everything around us trembled and shook. I held Lulu tightly and prayed as she buried her face into my chest.

'Hassan, I'm scared!' she screamed into my ear.

'Don't worry! I'm here, Lulu, I'm here!'

The helicopter dipped left and flew away. The wind died down and a sense of calm returned.

'They've gone,' I whispered. 'For now…'

***

That afternoon, we went to our neighbor Ahmed's house to see if he'd heard from our father. Ahmed's eyes were watery, his hair was messy and a faint smell of alcohol drifted from his purple lips. His nose was red and his brow was more wrinkled than normal. He saw that I had noticed his wet eyes and told us that the sand was making his eyes itch.

I knew the truth. Both of Ahmed's sons were military guards at a government building in Basra, in southern Iraq. I used to play with his two sons when I was younger. When they joined the military, Ahmed had thrown a large party and invited practically the whole neighborhood. Now they were fighting American troops.

'So, no word from our father?' I asked.

'No, and I haven't heard from my sons either,' Ahmed said. He wiped away a tear. 'This is all so horrible…'

Lulu grabbed my hand and told Ahmed that we would come back later. Before I could argue, she dragged me back towards our home.

'Hassan,' she said. 'I have something to show you.'

She led me through the front door and into the kitchen. From the drawer closest to the sink, she retrieved some letters. She smiled proudly, as if giving me the letters was part of some game we were playing. The top letter was dated from the previous week and addressed to me. I unfolded it and read it:

Hassan,

If you're reading this letter, it is because the Americans have attacked Baghdad and I haven't come home. Please take care of Lulu and wait for Uncle Sahir to come and get you. Do not try to find me. Do not go to the city. It's too dangerous. I'll see both of you soon. You must be strong, and you must look after Lulu.

Dad

I read the letter again. 'Why didn't you tell me about this letter earlier?' I asked. 'This is important!'

'Dad said to wait one day before I told you,' she said with a shrug. I felt crushed under the seriousness of our situation. *What were we supposed to do? How was I going to take care of Lulu?* I glanced down at the letter and at my father's signature.

I could almost feel him writing the letter. I looked at the final line: You must be strong, and you must look after Lulu.

'Let me read it, Hassan.'

'Don't worry. It says that our father is at the university, and if he isn't back here in one day, we will need to go and find him.' I hated lying to my sister, but I knew that I couldn't just wait around for our father to return. I folded the letters and put them in my back pocket.

'He wants us to go and find him?' Lulu asked, excited.

'Yes,' I said, walking away from her.

'Are we going to the city now?'

'Not just yet…' I answered over my shoulder. 'If he doesn't come home tonight, we will go tomorrow.'

'Hassan, have you tried calling Uncle Sahir?'

‘I tried this morning, but the phones were down.’

‘Try again,’ she said, bringing me the phone.

I picked up the telephone and dialed our uncle’s number. I waited for what felt like an eternity. ‘It’s not ringing.’

‘Call Dad’s university number,’ she suggested.

I dialed our father’s office number. Nothing. I hung up the phone and tried again, still no luck. ‘The phones must be down.’ I glanced down at my little sister. Her eyes were large and curious.

‘We will try again later,’ I assured her. ‘If we can’t reach them, we will go to the city. We will find Dad. Don’t worry, Lulu.’

The Thirteenth Chapter

A Mahoney Green Mystery

BY PATRICK KENNEDY

Prologue

The screech of car tyres, his heart beating, his footsteps on the cobbled streets. Were they just his footsteps or was there a second pair of footsteps behind him? No, just an echo. Where was he now? Not sure, but it looked familiar. He wasn't sure if that made him feel better or worse. They can't be from this city; that would be too much of a coincidence. They had been on the train. He was sure he was being followed on the train.

This looked promising, a church, maybe he could find a sympathetic priest who would help him; or at least somewhere to hide the Thirteenth Chapter. He searched for somewhere to hide his bag. Nowhere. He tried the door to the church. Locked. He went down the side of the church to some steps leading down to another cobbled street. Maybe it was the same street? He wasn't sure where he was; the adrenaline and lack of sleep made him confused.

Another screech of tyres. Closer this time. Definitely footsteps in the street. Sweat poured down his face and blinded him for a couple of seconds. He panicked and started running. It was dark in the churchyard. He ran straight into a wall. There was now a big cut on his head and his glasses were cracked and hanging off one ear. Blood and sweat combined into a salty, sticky mixture that flowed down his face. He could taste the blood in his mouth. Then he heard a familiar voice. He had heard the same voice on the train yesterday morning. The American.

He tried to go back the way he had come, but then he saw the figure of the other, shorter, man that was following him. He turned to run around the back of the church but something hit his already damaged forehead.

He could see the gold and white of the church against the black sky and then a face, a man's face with a scar on his cheek. He felt his bag being pulled from his hand. Then his eyes closed and the stars went out.

Chapter 1 – The Postcard

Mahoney looked at the postcard for about the twentieth time since it had arrived that morning. There was something about it that bothered her. Her father, Professor Montague Green (Monty to his friends), always sent her postcards from the places that he visited, but they were usually very long and full of information. He usually had to write very small so that he could put everything he wanted to say on the back of the card. This postcard, however, was very short and, to be honest, boring.

Monty had left England on another one of his trips three weeks before. Mahoney had received two other cards since then: one from Berlin Central Station (he only stopped there for an hour to change trains) and one from Moscow.

Professor Green was travelling through Europe to Russia by train. He was looking for what he called 'the missing chapter' of a book. Mahoney had no idea which book because her father didn't explain. This was also unusual, because he usually told Mahoney exactly where he was going and what he was looking for.

Monty Green was an expert on books, specifically old and rare books and manuscripts. He spent a lot of his time away from home, trying to track down books that had either been lost or may not even exist.

Just then, Mahoney's grandmother opened the door to her bedroom and came in carrying a tray of sandwiches, biscuits and tea. 'I thought you might be a bit hungry; you didn't eat much for dinner,' said Grandma as she put the tray down on the bed.

'Thanks, Gran.' Mahoney distractedly moved her red hair out of her face and pushed her glasses up her nose. She was still examining the postcard.

'What's that you're looking at?' asked Grandma, looking over Mahoney's shoulder. Grandma had a habit of reading over people's shoulders. She always did it on the bus, which Mahoney found very annoying and embarrassing.

'It's the postcard from Dad that arrived this morning,' said Mahoney, but she didn't sound like she usually did when she got a postcard from her father.

'Well, that's good, isn't it?' Grandma felt a little worried. She knew her granddaughter very well, so she could tell that something was wrong.

'I'm not so sure, Gran,' said Mahoney with a frown.

'Why not?' asked Grandma. 'It looks like any other postcard to me.'

'Yes, but does it really, Gran?' Mahoney turned round and held out the postcard for Grandma to look at.

‘Let’s have a look.’ Grandma took the card from Mahoney, put her glasses on and moved under the light. The writing on the back of the card said:

> Dear Mahoney,
>
> I’m having a great time here in Irkutsk. The scenery is lovely and the food is very nice. You be a good girl and help your grandma find me a nice Christmas present.
>
> Love Dad

After what felt like three hours, but was probably only three minutes, Grandma declared, ‘It is a bit short.’

‘Yes, Gran, it’s short and it’s boring,’ said Mahoney. ‘Also, look at the picture on the front.’

‘It’s just a building,’ said Grandma.

‘Exactly!’

Grandma was getting confused. She couldn’t really see why Mahoney was getting so excited about a postcard. ‘I’m sorry, Mahoney, but I’m a little lost now. What is so special about this postcard?’

‘The problem,’ said Mahoney, jumping up from the bed like she had got an electric shock, ‘is that the card is completely and utterly not special! Let’s look at the facts: one – there is a picture of Irkutsk Town Hall on the front, a very ugly and ordinary building; two – the message is short; three – the message is also boring; and four – it just doesn't sound like Dad.'

'Well, there is a reasonable explanation for all of those things, Mahoney.' Grandma sat down on the bed and pulled Mahoney down beside her so that she could calm her down.

'Really?'

'Yes, your dad was in a hurry, love,' said Grandma. 'He was probably busy and realized that he needed to send you a postcard, so he stopped at the nearest shop, bought a card, and quickly wrote something on the back. That's why it sounds a bit strange. Try not to worry, Mahoney. Your dad is an experienced traveller, he'll be fine.'

'OK, Gran,' said Mahoney. 'But I still think I'll get Woody to have a look at the postcard tomorrow.'

'OK then, but get some sleep now, it's getting late.' Grandma kissed Mahoney's freckly cheek.

The next morning, Mahoney got up later than she had planned, which made her a little angry. Mahoney didn't like feeling disappointed. She ate her tea and toast so fast that Grandma told her to slow down. She put on her brown hat, red coat and green gloves and ran across the park to Woody's house.

Woody lived about two hundred metres away. His house was across a small park with a duck pond in the middle. She usually stopped to give the ducks some bread, but today she was in a hurry. She got to Woody's front door less than a minute after she had closed her own front door behind her. She thought this might be a world record.

Woody's mother answered the door in her usual way: 'Oh, it's you.' Mahoney didn't like Woody's mother.

'Yes, that's right Mrs W, it's me. Is Woody in?' asked Mahoney politely. Woody's mother just opened the door and pointed upstairs. Mahoney didn't hang around to make conversation with Mrs W, she just ran up the stairs to Woody's room.

Mahoney opened the door without knocking because she knew it was pointless: Woody had been deaf since he was four years old. Woody didn't want to talk about how he had lost his hearing, so Mahoney never asked. She was very curious, though, and she secretly hoped that Woody was going to tell her how it had happened one day.

Mahoney burst through the door like a bank robber. Woody was so shocked that he fell off the bed and landed on the floor with a bang. This made Woody's mother shout up the stairs for them to 'keep the noise down.' Mahoney really didn't like Woody's mother… at all.

'Woody! I need your help,' said Mahoney excitedly.

'What's up?' said Woody in sign language as he got up from the floor.

'It's my dad.' Woody could read lips so Mahoney didn't need to use sign language, but she'd learned it so that she and Woody could communicate. Woody couldn't speak at all because he was so young when he lost his hearing.

'What about him? Is he OK?' Woody looked worried.

'I'm not sure. I want you to look at this postcard and tell me what you think.' Mahoney took the Irkutsk postcard from her old leather bag and gave it to Woody, who immediately grabbed a magnifying glass from the desk so that he could see the card properly. This is exactly what Mahoney had hoped for. Woody was good at science, so he always examined things very closely.

'Well? What do you think?' asked Mahoney impatiently.

'Do you have another postcard from your dad that I can compare this one to?' asked Woody.

'Yes, I do.' Mahoney reached into her bag and pulled out two more cards: the one from Berlin and the one from Moscow.

Woody had a good look at the cards, first without his magnifying glass and then with it. 'These two seem more natural, and they sound like your father, but this one doesn't seem like your father,' he said.

'I thought the same thing,' said Mahoney, nodding.

'But what does it mean?'

'I think it means that Dad is in trouble, and he's sending us a message that he wants us to help him.'

'Yes,' replied Woody, 'it even says 'help' in the message.'

'My goodness! You're right!' Mahoney grabbed the card from Woody's hand.

'Actually, it says 'help your grandma find me',' said Woody.

'Oh blimey! You're right! We have to go and look for my dad in Russia!'

'I don't think my mum will be too happy about that,' said Woody. 'She doesn't even like me walking to school on my own… and I'm sixteen years old.'

'Well my father needs us. Somebody has kidnapped him and forced him to write this postcard to me so that we think he's OK.'

'But why would anyone want to kidnap your dad?'

'I don't know, Woody... but I plan to find out.'

CPSIA information can be obtained
at www.ICGtesting.com
Printed in the USA
LVOW10s2347041217
558591LV00015BA/2301/P

9 781517 471132